T0196747

Jesus My Hope and Glory

Donovan Brown

IUNIVERSE, INC.
NEW YORK   BLOOMINGTON

Jesus My Hope and Glory

iUniverse books may be ordered through booksellers or by contacting:

iUniverse
1663 Liberty Drive
Bloomington, IN 47403
www.iuniverse.com
1-800-Authors (1-800-288-4677)

Because of the dynamic nature of the Internet, any Web addresses or links contained in this book may have changed since publication and may no longer be valid.

ISBN: 978-1-4401-3496-8 (pbk)
ISBN: 978-1-4401-3497-5 (ebk)

Printed in the United States of America

iUniverse rev. date: 3/30/2009

I love you Jesus my Lord and your love engulfs me.

Lord you have wrapped me up in your love.

Help me to know more about you, for you are wonderful and truly awesome.

Lord the beauty of your love for me is breathtaking, I want to know you more.

Jesus my Lord and God you are truly wonderful, hallowed be your name Lord, hallowed be the mighty name of Jesus, who is my Lord and God.

Amen

Lord Jesus you are greater than all my troubles,
my afflictions, my enemies and the powers of evil
which has launched an attack on my life.
Lord Jesus though these wars are launched against me
I surrender them to you, for these battles are not mine
to fight but they belong to you.
I know you have gone into my future and have
already defeated every foe who has come against me,
you have healed every sickness which has come upon
me and have already solved all the problems and
troubles I face.
I shout in advance that all my troubles are over and I
declare victory mine over them all in the name of Jesus.
Thank you Lord Jesus my saviour, Amen.

Satan you and all the powers of evil are defeated
in my life and in my home in the name of Jesus.
Satan your attack on me has made me stronger and
greater than I was before your vicious attacks.
Satan you and the powers of darkness and evil are my
defeated foes in the name of Jesus.
Victory is mine in the mighty name of Jesus, amen.

Lord Jesus you told me to pray for my leaders,
so Lord I present the leaders of this nation to you.
Lord take control of their lives and mind and lead them
and cause them to do your will here on earth.
Lord Jesus, give them the vision, wisdom, knowledge
and understanding they need to govern well.
Surround them with officials and advisors who are
under your control and influence.
Lord Jesus I leave this government in your hands to
rule and lead.
It is in the name of Jesus that I pray, amen.

This is a blessed day, this is a glorious day.
Lord Jesus my King and my God thank you for blessing
me to live in this day.
You have given me new strength, good health and have
endowed me with power to defeat the powers of evil.
You Lord have me surrounded with your angels for them
to protect and to provide for me.
Jesus my Lord you have brought joy to my life and your
peace overflows within me.
Lord if it was not for your mercy and love for me I
would not have seen this day, thank you Lord for
your mercy and love.
In the name of Jesus I pray, amen.

Lord Jesus I lift my hands to praise you, how good and wonderful you are to me, thank you for being in my life.

Hallelujah Jesus, Mighty God.

Where there was turmoil in my life you have brought peace; where there was defeat you have brought victory; where there was sadness you brought great joy.

Lord Jesus you are magnificent and wonderful and I praise you Lord for you have brought great peace, joy and happiness to my life.

Lord Jesus out of your great love you sought me and brought me out of darkness into your kingdom, despite my many faults and sins committed.

Jesus my Lord you are truly wonderful and excellent, in the name of Jesus I pray amen.

Holy Spirit thank you for hearing my prayers and coming into my life and the gifts and favours which you have brought from the kingdom of heaven into my life which has truly enriched me greatly.

Thank you for the opportunities you have led me to, the problems you have resolved, the wounds which you have healed and the grace and mercy I have received.

Holy Spirit thank you for the spirits of darkness and evil which you have cast out of my life and out of my home.

Spirit of the true and living God you have come in your power and authority and have brought me great peace, joy, prosperity and authority. Holy Spirit thank you for coming and for what you have brought into my life and for what you have done for me.

Hallelujah Holy Spirit, Spirit of the one true and living God. In Jesus name, amen.

Lord Jesus thank you for your Holy Spirit and your blood.
Lord your Holy Spirit lives in me and your blood covers me.
Jesus my King hallelujah.

Mighty God because your Spirit lives in me, my spoken
words have authority and power. Because your Holy Spirit
lives in me I can speak life to death, healing to sickness,
victory to defeat and it will be done.

Lord Jesus as you have endowed me with awesome power,
I ask you to give me wisdom and understanding to speak
wisely and to your glory.

In the name of Jesus I ask and pray, amen.

Lord Jesus there are two ways that I can go through this storm. I can either go through it anxious, depressed, screaming and worried or I can go through it by casting all my cares on you and go to sleep resting I your peace. Knowing and believing that when this is all over things will be much better and brighter than they were before.

Lord you have allowed this storm to come into my life at this time for a good reason, so I choose to leave all in your hands and rest in your peace. Knowing your will is being done and I will come out as pure gold in the end.

Thank you Jesus my King and Lord for giving me your peace during this storm and for my the victory and blessings at the end of it all.

Hallelujah Jesus, thank you Lord my King.

In the name of Jesus that I pray, amen.

Jesus my Lord and Almighty God, you have given me this
day. It is a beautiful day filled with your love, favour,
mercy, grace and blessings for me.

Lord Jesus I surrender myself into your loving arms.

Be with me throughout today; wrap me up in your loving
arms; direct, council and protect me and my loved ones
throughout today.

Lord Jesus you are wonderful and I love you Lord.

In the name of Jesus I pray, amen.

Lord Jesus you are magnificent and excellent you are truly wonderful and excellent Lord. Hallelujah Jesus you are truly worthy of my honour and praise.

There is so much darkness in this world but you have brought so much beauty and light and life into my life. Jesus you are truly wonderful and excellent, Lord Jesus you are truly wonderful and excellent.

Hallowed be the name of Jesus, you are worthy of my praise. It is in the name of Jesus that I pray, amen.

Satan you and the forces of darkness and the powers of evil
has launched a merciless attack on my life.
But I declare in the name of Jesus that I will not die but
instead I will live and declare the goodness and the power
and glory of Almighty God.
In the name of Jesus, amen.

Lord Jesus you are my refuge and my strength.
You are my mountain mover and my deliverer; you are my light and my guide in this world.
Lord Jesus the powers of evil has launched a devastating attack on the one I love. They have brought chaos, confusion, pain and suffering to the one who is close to my heart.
Lord Jesus I am powerless to help so I turn to you Lord for help. It is impossible for you to fail you are the conquering Christ, you are my champion.
Lord Jesus please step in and release my darling from this impossible situation and from the grasp of the powers of evil; for in your presence there are no impossibilities.
Lord Jesus I thank you in advance for what you have already done for me and my loved one in the future.
Thank you for setting my loved one free from the bondage of evil.
Thank you Lord, in the name of Jesus that I pray, amen.

Lord Jesus you are mine and I am yours and nothing can separate me from your love.

You came into my life and have made me more than a thousand times better than I was and blessed me.

Lord Jesus you are mine and I am yours, your blood and Spirit testifies that I am a child of our Father in heaven and your wounds bears the evidence of the price you have paid for me.

Hallelujah Jesus, you are the High, true and living God.

Hallelujah my Lord and God, it is in the name of Jesus that I pray, amen.

Holy Spirit you have come into my life in your power and authority and have removed every mountain which had stood before me. You have destroyed every yoke which the enemy had placed on me and opened every door to bless me.

You have fed me with the word of truth and which has renewed my mind, setting my thoughts free to believe that Christ Jesus will do for me that which is impossible.

Holy Spirit thank you for the freedom which you have brought me, the burdens which you have lifted, the demons you have cast out of my life, the battles won for me and the victories you have given to me.

Holy Spirit thank you for the promises and the answers you have brought from heaven and manifested them in my life. Thank you for bringing me into this great wealth where I am free and far from poverty and lack.

Holy Spirit thank you, are awe-inspiring and wonderful, hallelujah. In Jesus name, amen.

Lord Jesus you were destined to suffer and die on the cross and you hand picked Judas knowing that he would betray you. But when your sufferings was over and you rose from the dead you were given all authority in heaven and on earth and over everything in the spiritual as well as in the natural realm.

You even took the keys of death and hell and authority from Satan. Judas was an important part of your destiny.

So Lord I believe that these troubles which you have allowed to come into my life is not to kill me but to propel me into the destiny which you have ordained for me. You and I know that you have destined me to prosper and be in good health even as my soul prospers.

So I thank you for leading me into the destiny you have prepared in advance for me.

In the name of Jesus I pray, amen.

Lord Jesus you have been so good and faithful to me.
It is your love, grace and mercy for me which has
brought me into this day.
Lord Jesus truly you are a loving and merciful God, for I
have not earned your favour and mercy but you have given
them so freely and lavishly to me.
So many times have I walked away from you and disobeyed
you, yet you have never left my side of forsook me.
I feel safe and I find security in knowing you are with me.
Lord Jesus please forgive me of all the sins which I have
committed and please council and lead me.
It is in the name of Jesus that I ask and pray, amen.

Lord Jesus you had allowed the forces of evil to invade my life. You allowed the attacks so that I would run to you and you would lead me into the wealth which you had prepared for me.

Lord you allowed Satan to attack and take away all that you had blessed Job with but in the end, after all his sufferings and troubles were over you blessed him with more than he ever had before.

You allowed David to encounter Goliath which brought him wealth and fame when the fight was over.

Lord you have allowed these troubles to come upon me so that you can promote me on earth and grow in the spiritual.

Thank you for not allowing more trouble than I can endure to come upon me, and thank you for using these troubles to bring me into the wealth and blessings which you have prepared for me here on earth. It is in the name of Jesus that I pray and thank you Lord, amen.

Lord Jesus please come into my life and put the shattered pieces of my life together again. Lord my life at this moment is shattered and I need you to help me to bring order to my life and rejoin the shattered pieces of my life together again.

Lord Jesus come in and bring order and peace to my life and into my home, I need your help now Lord. In the name of Jesus I ask and pray, amen.

Lord Jesus eyes have not seen and ears have not heard neither has it entered into the harts of men what you have prepared for me. Father I can feel it in my spirit that good and great changes are coming to my life, Lord I can feel in my spirit that my promotion is coming.

Thank you Jesus, hallelujah Lord.

I can feel it in my spirit that your promises to bless and prosper me are being birthed at this very moment, Jesus thank you Lord, this is my moment, this is the beginning of my lifetime of prosperity.

Lord Jesus you have already done it in the supernatural and it is now happening in the natural and no devil or powers of evil can stop this.

Hallelujah Jesus, thank you Lord.

It is in the name of Jesus that I pray and give thanks, amen.

Lord Jesus I am guided and protected by you.
Though war may breakout against me I will not be defeated
or be moved, for you have defeated my enemies for my
sake.
It is evident that I am blessed and highly favoured by you
Lord Jesus. Though my troubles maybe many you will bring
me safely through them all.
Lord you have taken away the powers of my enemies to
hurt me. I am truly blessed and highly favoured by you
Jesus my Lord. I am truly blessed and favoured by you,
thank you Lord.
It is in the name of Jesus that I pray, amen.

Holy Spirit, wonderful and beautiful Holy Spirit.
You have come into my home and have destroyed
every yoke which the powers of evil had over the
minds of my family members and myself. You have
freed us from the bondage of the powers of evil and
darkness.
Spirit of the true and living God, you have destroyed
the limitations which evil had placed in our minds
concerning our lives and future. You have helped us to
believe that all things are possible to them who
believe in Christ Jesus.
Hallelujah Holy Spirit, you are truly great and wonderful.
Hallelujah Spirit of the true and living God,
you have brought freedom, peace, hope, victory and
happiness to me and my family.
In Jesus name, amen.

Jesus my King you have crowned me with victory and everywhere I go I conquer in you name.

The enemies which have come against me will scatter and flee my presence. They are powerless to harm or defeat me for your Holy Spirit lives within me, your blood covers me and your love surrounds me.

Lord Jesus wherever I go I will conquer, wherever I go I will prosper and whatever I do is destined to prosper because you are with me and in your presence there is no failure or impossibilities. Lord Jesus my King hallelujah, you are truly wonderful and awesome.

It is in the name of Jesus that I pray, amen.

Lord Jesus thank you for holding me together during this tough and dark time. Thank you for holding my mind together and thank you for holding my family together.
Lord Jesus thank you for the peace and hope you have given and assurance that we will make it safely through this tough and dark time.
These sufferings will not last forever and I am confident that you will see us through safely.
I am confident that my family and I will get through this safely for my hope and trust is in you Lord. I am confident that you will never leave or forsake us. Jesus you are my help and my hope in you will not be disappointed.
Thank you Lord, in the name of Jesus I pray, amen.

Hallelujah Jesus my Lord, hallelujah Jesus my King
Hallelujah Jesus my provider, hallelujah Jesus my deliverer
Hallelujah Jesus my way-maker, hallelujah Jesus my
mountain mover, Jesus you are excellent and wonderful
and you are truly awesome.
Jesus my King, Jesus my Lord, Jesus my God, hallelujah.
My God you are truly awesome, Jesus my God you are
truly excellent.
My help comes from you Lord; my strength comes from
you, my victories over and in all things comes from you.
Jesus my God, hallelujah.
Lord you are truly wonderful and excellent, in Jesus name I
speak and believe this, amen.

Lord Jesus I come boldly to your thrown of grace,
power and authority.
Lord I am being attacked on all sides, but I will not worry
for I believe you will bring me trough safely and
victoriously.
Lord I do not know how you are going to deliver me I
only have to believe that you will and the rest is
up to you. You have delivered me out of these troubles in
the twinkle of an eye.
Within the twinkling of an eye all my troubles are gone, all
barriers which hindered me from my blessings are
demolished and doors ot wonderful opportunities are
opened in my life in the name of Jesus.
Lord Jesus you have done it many times before and you will
do it many more times again in the name of Jesus.
It is in the name of Jesus that I pray and thank you Lord,
amen.

Lord Jesus you inhabit the praise of your people.
So I am will praise you because when you are present
in my life every problem affecting my life is be solved,
every good thing which died in my life is resurrected.

In your presence Lord every need is be met,
every cursed broken, every enemy defeated and every
demon flees.
Lord in your presence there is life, peace, joy, help, hope,
love, healing, victory, deliverance, prosperity and
happiness.
Lord Jesus I praise you and I thank you for meeting my
every need and giving me the desires of my heart.
It is in the name of Jesus that I pray and thank you Lord,
amen.

Lord Jesus my God I lift up my hands to praise,
I lift up my hands to worship you; I lift up my hands to
honour you, because you have done it again.
You have delivered me, you have blessed me, and you have
honoured your word to helped me.
Yes Lord you have done it again, you have taken all my
troubles and have given me victory over them all. You have
fought all my battles and given me the victories.
Jesus my Lord truly there is no one else like you, none so
faithful and kind.
Jesus my King you have done great things for me yet again.
Hallelujah Jesus, thank you Lord for you have blessed me,
healed m, helped me and have delivered me safely yet
again.
Thank you Lord, it is in the name of Jesus that I give thanks
and pray, amen.

Jesus, Lord Jesus I praise you,
I lift you up for you have done great things
in my life, you have done awesome things in my life.
You have performed the impossible for me.
Lord your glory is risen upon me and your Spirit is at work
within and around me.
Jesus Lord there is no one else like you and I am excited
and honoured that you are in my life.
Jesus hallelujah my God, you are good, Lord you are
wonderful and I am glad that your Holy Spirit resides in me.
Lord you have glorified me and have set me free from the
powers of evil.
Jesus my God you are incredible, my God you are amazing,
Lord you are wonderful.
Hallelujah Jesus, King of heaven and glory.
In the name of Jesus I pray, amen.

Lord Jesus thank you for my job for it provides me with the money that I need to pay my bills. Lord I am truly grateful for it but Lord I need and desire greater financial wealth and power.

Lord it is you who gives the power and ability to create wealth, so Lord I come boldly to your thrown and ask in the name of Jesus that you give me the power and opportunities to create great wealth. So that I can live in financial dominion and prosperity and that I will be able to richly bless others more than I can bless them currently.

Lord Jesus, please help me to use the talents which you have deposited in me and use the opportunities which you have created for me to bring me into financial prosperity and dominion.

It is in the name of Jesus that I ask, amen

Lord Jesus the same Spirit which you used to raise Lazarus from the dead lives in me. Lord the same Spirit you used to heal the woman with the issue of blood lives in me.

Jesus the same Spirit that you used to cast the legion of demons out of the man into the pigs lives in me.

Lord the same Holy Spirit that you used to feed five thousand people with five loves and two fishes lives in me.

Lord Jesus the same Spirit which you used to turn water into wine lives in me.

Lord because your Holy Spirit lives in me I can speak life to death and it will be accomplished. Jesus because you Spirit lives in me I can speak healing to sickness and it will be accomplished. Lord because your Holy Spirit lives in me I can speak victory to defeat and it will be accomplished.

Lord Jesus thank you for your Holy Spirit which lives in me and your glory which is shining upon me.

Hallelujah Jesus, thank you Lord for giving me you Holy Spirit.

In the name of Jesus I pray, amen.

Jesus my Lord, God and King you are my saviour

Jesus you are my mountain mover,

Jesus you are my way-maker, Jesus you are my deliverer.

Lord no one else in the world can do what you can do Lord.

You are my help; my help comes from you Lord.

Hallelujah Jesus my God, hallelujah Jesus my deliverer

Hallelujah Jesus my provider

Hallelujah Jesus, you are awesome,

Lord you are awe-inspiring

You are amazing, you are wonderful

Lord you are incredible; no one else can do what
you can do, and no one else could do for me what you
have done for me.

Jesus my King hallelujah, thank you Lord.

It is in the name of Jesus I pray, amen.

Lord Jesus had it not been for your love and mercy my troubles would have killed me they would have destroyed me. Even I thought there was no hope and believed that there was no way out of my troubles. I believed it was the end for me; I had even dug my own grave and waited for my troubles to destroy me.

But Jesus my Lord you had not given up on me, you had not abandoned me, you Lord came to my rescue . To my amazement you showed up unexpectedly and solved all my troubles and defeated every enemy which had come against me.

Lord I declare that you have done the impossible for me, had you not showed up and acted on my behalf I would have died. I would have been utterly consumed by my troubles.

My God you are awesome. Lord you rescued me from death and destruction and blessed me.

Hallelujah Jesus, Lord you are amazing, Lord you are incredible.

Thank you Lord, it is in the name of Jesus that I pray, amen.

Abba Father and Almighty God I come to you in the name of Jesus. Father you delight in the success and prosperity of your children. Father you want me to live in abundance of all good things so much that you ordained and sent your only begotten son Jesus from glory to teach me and to suffer and die for me to live in abundance of all good things here on earth and have eternal life with you. So Father I ask you in the name of Jesus to lead me into my wealth which you have stored on this earth for me. Stir up the talents that you have deposited in me and give me the opportunities and resources that will allow me to use these talents which will bring great financial and material wealth to my life.

It is in the name of Jesus that I ask, amen.

Abba Father in heaven I feel so afraid Lord, so please hold me tight into your loving arms and encourage me with your Holy Spirit and lift me up.

Father you know what I need so please bless me now with what I need. I find peace in you, I find peace in talking to you; I find great peace in telling you about what is troubling me.

Father because of your love for me you have resolved all my worries and have healed me.

Heavenly Father thank you for the great privilege of being able to enter into your presence and receive your great love.

Abba Father you are truly wonderful and I am grateful that you are present in my life.

It is in the name of Jesus that I pray, amen.

Jehovah my Father you have made me whole again.
Father you have made my life whole again. Mighty God
you have made my life whole again.

Father you have reconnected the pieces of my life which
was scattered, the pieces of my life which the enemy had
separated. Abba Father by your Holy Spirit you have made
me whole again, you are truly amazing.

It is you who give sight to those who were blind, it is you
who give life to the those who were dead, it is you who
make the lame walk and it is you who deliver your people
out of all their troubles.

Father I look to you for help and I come to you for help,
my help comes from you Lord my God.

Mighty God you have done great things for me, great and
wonderful things; hallowed be the name of Jehovah
the Most High God.

In Jesus name I, amen.

Jehovah Almighty God and Father I come to your thrown of grace and power in the name of Jesus, to give you thanks for sending your Holy Spirit into my life, who has cleaned up all the mess which I got myself into and all the troubles which had invaded my life.

Father I stand before you a living testament of your love and faithfulness. Your love penetrated the kingdom of darkness and brought me into your kingdom of power, light and eternal life. Father I am shining in the light of you glory for your glory has risen upon me.

Father and Eternal God thank you for your love and Great Spirit which is in me and is working for me.

It is in the name of Jesus that I pray, amen.

This is a great day, this is a wonderful day.
I have new strength, good health and peace of mind.
Jesus my God thank you for this day, this day filled with
victory and power. I am empowered this day by your
Holy Spirit, I will prosper today, I will conquer today, I will
declare your goodness in this day. I am blessed with
knowledge, empowered wisdom and you have blessed
me with understanding and gifted with vision.
No weapon created to harm me in anyway will prosper,
in the name of Jesus I declare victory over my enemies and
every weapon that is built to harm me.
Blessed be the name of the Lord, blessed be the name of
Jesus. In the name of Jesus I declare this, amen.

Lord Jesus I am not going to wait for my blessings to come before I praise you, Lord I will praise you from now.

For my faith in you tells me that you have already blessed me, even though there is no evidence at present. Even though all looks lost, even though all looks hopeless; but Lord my eyes are not focused on this storm but instead I am focused on you.

You are faithful and you have promised to deliver me from all my worries and bless me and you will satisfy my heart's desire. I know you have already done it Lord, I do not need to see it to believe it. So I lift up my hands to praise and worship you now for victory is mine in the end over these present and future troubles. I believe it and declare it so in the name of Jesus.

Thank you Lord, in the name of Jesus I pray, amen.

Hell has been let loose in my life.

My life seems doomed for destruction, but Lord Jesus I know you are with me and as long as you are with me I can rejoice in this storm; for troubles can only last for I while. Lord Jesus you are faithful and just, Lord if I was not able to handle these troubles you would not have allowed them to come upon me, if you had not given me power over them Lord you would not have allowed them to enter my life.

This is why I know I already have the victory over these Troubles. Though the winds may howl and the clouds look ominous and the waves overpowering and my boat seems doomed I know that I will live and declare your goodness and love and glory when this storm ceases to exist even in memory.

My eyes are focused on you Lord, not the storm, my faith is in you which give you the authority to act on my behalf. Thank you Lord for your goodness, love and faithfulness to me. It is in the name of Jesus that I pray, amen

The Holy Spirit of the Lord is upon me and is within me, and

he has anointed me to preach the gospel to the poor; he has sent me to heal the broken-hearted, and to preach deliverance to the captives, and recover sight to the blind, and to set free them that are bound.

It is in the name of Jesus that I declare this, amen.

Lord Jesus is life worth living without someone to love and to receive love from?

Lord you told me that it is not good for man\woman to be alone and that you will make a suitable companion for him\her.

I am in agreement with you Lord that it is not good for man\woman to be alone, I am alone Lord, so please bring into my life right now the life long companion whom you have created for me to share my life with and to be my wife\husband. It is in the name of Jesus that I ask according to your word and promise. In Jesus name, amen.

Ministering angels of Jesus the Lord of hosts go
to the east and to the west, to the north and to
the south and bring into my life all the treasures which is
stored on this earth for me. Do this now in the name of
Jesus.
Ministering angels of Jesus the Lord of hosts bring back into
my life all which the forces of evil has stolen from me, do
this now in the name of Jesus.

Lord Jesus thank you for blessing me, my life is filled with your blessings right now, you have even gone into my future and blessed me.

Lord even though my future blessings have not yet manifested I thank and praise you for them now,

Lord my best days on this earth are yet to come because of what you have done for me in advance.

Jesus King of heaven, Great and Mighty God, hallelujah.

Lord you are wonderful and faithful to me;

Lord you are great and wonderful.

Hallelujah Jesus my Lord you are worthy of my praise and worship for what you have done for me in the past, present and future, thank you Jesus my King.

It is in the name of Jesus that I pray, amen.

Holy Spirit you penetrated the kingdom of death and evil and invaded my life and changed my life by renewing my mind with the word of God.

You have brought me into the kingdom of eternal life, Holy Spirit I ask you in the name of Jesus to do the same for my brothers and sisters, my mother and father, my aunts and uncles and my cousins and friends.

Enter their lives Holy Spirit and renew their minds with the word of Almighty God and lead them into His kingdom of light, victory, glory and eternal life and joy.

It is in the name of Jesus that I ask and pray, amen.

Lord Jesus you said if I bring the tithe to you, you Lord would rebuke the powers of evil for my sake and you would open the windows of heaven and pour out a blessing in my life I will not have room enough to receive it all.

Lord my God as I have been obedient to your instructions you have been faithful to you promises and have rebuked the enemy and bound the powers of evil out of my life for my sake. You have given me financial dominion; you have blessed my family with your favour, your protection, good health, with good jobs, businesses, great opportunities and you have blessed me with a wonderful wife\husband. You have blessed me with success so that where ever I go and whatever I do you cause me to prosper.

Lord Jesus thank you for being faithful to your promises made to me.

In Jesus name I pray, amen.

As you have promised Lord, that weeping may endure for the night but my joy will come in the morning.

Hallelujah Jesus it is morning and my joy has come, my joy has come in the name of Jesus, my joy has come.

My weeping is over, my pain is over, my sufferings are over and my waiting is over. Hallelujah Jesus you have brought me great joy, it is morning and my joy has come, Jesus hallelujah.

I cried all night, I waited all night, I suffered all night, I prayed all night and now it is morning you Lord Jesus my God has brought me great joy.

Hallelujah Jesus you have given me beauty for ashes, the oil of joy for mourning, the garment of praise for the spirit of heaviness, new strength, victory, power, promotions and peace.

Hallelujah Jesus it is morning and you have brought me great joy and blessings.

It is in the name of Jesus that I declare this and pray, amen.

Thank you for this day Lord Jesus, thank you for blessing me with new strength and good health. Lord Jesus be with me throughout today, please lead and guide me. Please Lord I ask in the name of Jesus that you protect me and give me your favour. Give me new ideas and opportunities to generate wealth so that I will prosper financially. Help me to recognise these opportunities no matter how small and insignificant they may seem help me to use them wisely.

Lord Jesus thank you for good health and for clothing me in a right frame of mind.

Thank you Lord it is in the name of Jesus that I ask and pray, amen.

Satan, you and all powers of darkness the blood of
Jesus is against you. I plead the blood of Jesus upon
my life and over everyone and thing which belongs to me.
I plead the blood of Jesus over my family, my job/business,
and over my finance.
I rebuke you Satan and the powers of evil in the name of
Jesus; and I bind your presence and you work out of my
life, out of my family, out of my neighbourhood, out of my
business/ my job and out of my finances.
I declare in the name of Jesus my victory over you and the
powers of evil and your plans and works.

I have sinned throughout today Lord Jesus,
please forgive me as I come into your presence.
Lord I thank you for taking care of not only me but also my
family throughout today. Thank you for not only blessing
me but also my family.
Lord Jesus please watch over us tonight, protect us from
evil and speak to us as we sleep.
Thank you Lord Jesus my Lord and God,
in Jesus name I pray, amen.

I will get through these storms,

Jesus will bring me safely through these troubles.

I will go through these troubles in perfect peace.

Lord Jesus you have brought me through many storms safely and victoriously before, no matter how violent they were or impossible they seemed to me.

Lord Jesus I leave in your hands every charge that the enemy has brought against me. Lord I leave in your hands ever action the enemy has taken against me. Lord Jesus I leave ever evidence the enemy has brought against me. I leave in your hands Lord Jesus ever witness that the enemy has brought against me. Lord Jesus I leave myself and my enemies in your hands.

Jesus my God I love you Lord, hallelujah Jesus, thank you for my victories over my enemies and troubles and for the peace and great joy you have given me.

It is in the name of Jesus that I pray, amen.

Lord Jesus the desire for me to be financially prosperous is not a sin. Lord you have commanded me to be prosperous, you told me to have dominion over the earth and you have promised to bless and prosper me wherever I go and cause whatever I do to prosper. You told me it is you who gives the power to create wealth.

Lord Jesus help me to birth a business and help me to run it successfully so that it will bring me great financial rewards. Lord thank you for the people whom you have into my life who will help me to achieve this, thank you for the doors of opportunities you have opened for me to achieve this.

Lord Jesus thank you for providing me with the resources, wisdom, knowledge and vision to bring this successful company into reality.

It is in the name of Jesus I pray and thank you in advance Lord for what you have done for me to help me to bring my company into reality, in Jesus name, amen.

Lord Jesus you have created me to be in union with a member of the opposite sex. For you said that it is not good for a man to be alone and you will make a companion suitable for him. Lord Jesus you have blessed me with a burning passion only this person can truly quench and you have created a void in me only that person can truly fit.

So Lord Jesus I ask in accordance to your word that you bring right now into my life, the life long companion whom you have created to rid me of loneliness, filling this empty void and quenching this burning passion which I have. I sincerely ask this in the name of Jesus.

Lord Jesus thank you for answering my prayer by bringing this wonderful person in my life, who is truly a blessing and a gift from you to me, Lord.

Hallelujah Jesus my King wonderful merciful God, thank you for this precious gift.

In Jesus name I thank you Lord for my wife/husband, thank you Jesus, thank you Lord, amen.

Holy Spirit of the true and living God,
the powers of evil are fighting me on my job and in my
home.
They have brought confusion, division and malice.
Holy Spirit in the name of Jesus come now in your power
and move in your authority and exterminate the threats of
the enemy, uproot and cast out the spirits of evil which has
invaded my home and my place of work.
Holy Spirit in the name of Jesus act now and defend my
family, release them from the control of the enemy.
Holy Spirit crush and cast out the powers of evil which have
invaded my place of work.
Holy Spirit act now in the name of Jesus I ask and pray,
amen.

Lord Jesus I don't have to wait for my blessings to come for you are here, I don't have to wait for my miracle to come for you are here, I don't have to wait for my deliverance to come for you are here.

I don't have to wait for my healing to come for you are here.

You Lord are my blessing, you are my miracle, you are my deliverer, you are my provider, you are my help, you Lord are my healer.

Because you are with me Lord every mountain before me is be levelled, ever barrier which separates me from every good thing is removed and all my enemies are defeated because you are with me.

Jesus my faith is in you alone, my hope I place in you I am certain that I will not be disappointed.

Jesus Great and Mighty God, hallelujah, you are here and by your Spirit you are doing great and marvellous things for me and through me.

In Jesus name, amen.

Lord Jesus I must praise you Lord, for the only reason why I am here in this day is simply because of your grace and mercy.

Lord Jesus I must praise you Lord, for the only reason why I am here in this day is simply because of your unconditional love for me which I have not earned but have been freely given.

Lord Jesus hallelujah my God, Jesus Lord hallelujah.

Lord I sin consciously but you are still with me, clothing me in your unconditional love.

Jesus Mighty God, hallelujah, it is truly amazing that you who created everything out of nothing can love me so unconditionally who has so many flaws.

Jesus you are a Holy God and yet you love me so greatly even though I give in to sin so willingly at times.

Jesus my God you are true wonderful, hallelujah, Jesus, Great and mighty God.

In Jesus name I pray and give you thanks Lord, amen.

Lord Jesus thank you for your favour, your grace and unconditional love for me.

You are wonderful and truly amazing.

Hallelujah, Lord you are worthy of my praise.

My Jesus you have blessed me with a prosperous present and future, I am shining in the light of your glory even now.

Lord what my enemies have brought against me to destroy me you have caused it to bless me instead. You have used my enemies to bless me so that I can be a blessing to others.

Jesus you are so wonderful, Lord you are so awesome.

My God, hallelujah, holy and merciful God, hallelujah.

Lord I sometimes overlook good health as being a blessing, I sometimes take the ability to walk, see and speak and hear for granted. I sometimes overlook the ability to live a normal life as being a blessing, but Lord I am truly blessed. Thank you for blessing my life completely and the privilege of your presence in my life.

In Jesus name, amen.

Hallelujah Jesus Great and Mighty God,
Lord you have done great things for me.
Jesus please forgive me of the sins which I have
committed.
Jesus my saviour and King you have brought me from
a place where I had little into a place where I live in
abundance of all good things. Lord you have
completely turned my life around.
Jesus my Lord and Great God you took me out of hell
and have seated me on a thrown in heaven with you.
Jesus, Great and Mighty King you have given me victory
after victory over my enemies both those in the
natural as well as in the supernatural realms.
Jesus my King you are the Conquering Christ.
Hallelujah Jesus my Great King.
Speak to me Lord and lead me always, in the name of
Jesus I ask and pray, amen.

Lord Jesus you allowed me to be thrown into a deep dark pit and then allowed me to be enslaved, then thrown into a cold and lonely prison while you had all power to help me and set me free. It was if all my prayers to you had fallen on deaf ears and my cries for help were all in vain.

Then at the right time, your time, at your chosen moment you Lord brought me out of prison into the light, into the palace into the very presence and glory of Almighty God.

Lord you took me out of tragedy into triumph, from complete defeat to absolute victory, from no hope into your glory and from anonymity into great authority.

Jesus Mighty God hallelujah, you have turned my life completely around and have given me new strength, new joy peace and prosperity.

Hallelujah Lord Jesus my Great and Mighty King.

Looking back Lord I can see why you had allowed me to be thrown into the pit, to be enslaved by others falsely accused and imprisoned. It was to prepare me for a destiny you had prepared for me, a bright and prosperous future which I am now living in today.

Hallelujah Jesus, my Great and Mighty King.

In Jesus name, amen.

Abba Father in heaven thank you for your love
and devotion to me. Father you sent your innocent son
Jesus to suffer and die an agonizing and humiliating death
for me, for sins I have committed. Father you watched him
being humiliated and suffer and die on a crossed and
descended into hell, cursed and separated from you for my
sake. But you were in him and through him you reconciled
not only me but those who accept him as Lord and saviour
of their life. You raised Christ Jesus from the dead and gave
him all power and authority over everything in heaven and
earth and you seated us on a thrown in heaven in him.
Giving us eternal access into your very presence.
Father please forgive me of the sins which I have
committed and Jesus is my Lord and Saviour.
Abba Father, hallelujah.
Thank you Father in Jesus name, amen.